DREAM WEAVER
Advanced Creative Writing Prompts for Storytellers

First Edition
2024
Independently published

For E and K,
who inspire me.

Dear Writer,

In your hands is a key to worlds where imagination knows no bounds and creativity reigns supreme. This book is your gateway to endless possibilities, crafted especially for the great storyteller within you.

Dive into a treasure trove of writing prompts spanning genres like a vibrant palette waiting to be explored. Let them be your guiding stars as you navigate the vast universe of storytelling. Use them as sparks to ignite your imagination and as compasses to steer your stories toward new horizons.

Embrace the joy of storytelling with every fiber of your being. Let your imagination soar, allow your words to dance on the page, and let your stories touch hearts and inspire minds. The world is waiting to be enchanted by your stories, so go ahead and start weaving your next masterpiece!

S. J. Harker

Before You Start

Are you ready to dive into the world of prompts and discover how they can fuel your creativity and inspire your storytelling? Let's explore practical tips to help you harness the power of prompts and transform them into captivating stories.

First, read through the prompts with an open mind. Let your imagination roam freely. Don't feel pressured to choose a prompt right away—take your time to explore each one. Pay attention to the ones that immediately spark your interest or curiosity. Trust your instincts—they're your compass in this creative journey.

Once you've selected a prompt, take a moment to brainstorm ideas. Write down everything that comes to mind—plot twists, character sketches, settings, and themes. Let your thoughts flow without judgment.

Sometimes, the wildest ideas can lead to the most intriguing stories. Use this brainstorming session to build a solid foundation for your narrative. The more you immerse yourself in the world of your story, the more authentic and compelling your narrative will become.

Consider approaching the prompt from different angles. Think about how you can add a unique twist or spin to the initial idea. Experiment with possibilities and let your creativity shine.

Having a roadmap helps you stay focused and ensures your story unfolds smoothly. However, don't be afraid to deviate from your outline if new ideas emerge during the writing process.

Don't be afraid to revise and refine your story. The first draft is just the beginning—editing is where the magic happens. Polish your prose, tighten your plot, and fine-tune your dialogue. Consider feedback from trusted friends, family, or writing groups to help you identify areas for improvement. Remember, great stories often undergo multiple revisions before they shine brightly.

Lastly, enjoy the process of writing. Embrace the joy of storytelling and let your passion for writing shine through in every word. Celebrate your achievements, both big and small, and stay motivated on your journey to becoming an accomplished author. Remember, every story you write is a stepping stone toward realizing your dreams.

So, dear writer, seize the opportunity to make the most of the writing prompts in this book. Use them as tools to ignite your imagination, expand your storytelling repertoire, and craft stories that captivate and inspire.

Your creative journey starts here—embrace it with enthusiasm and let your stories soar! Happy writing, and may your adventures in storytelling be filled with endless inspiration and discovery!

"Through words, we weave entire worlds, where imagination dances and dreams take flight, painting the canvas of possibility with the strokes of our pen."

SJ Harker

PROMPT #1
An aspiring writer
is haunted by a
ghostly muse who
inspires him to
write great stories
but also demands
payment in blood.

PROMPT #2

A teenager with a stutter accidentally summons a malevolent demon while practicing Latin for a test. The demon tries to force the teenager to fulfill three deadly tasks for him, only to find out that the teenager is not who she seems to be.

PROMPT #3

A young architect inherits plans for a magical city, realizing she is the heir to an architect's guild protected by construct guardians against a rogue kingdom seeking to exploit the city's magic.

PROMPT #4
A girl cursed to
turn into a
dragon must
battle her own
monstrous form
each night to
protect her
village from
herself.

PROMPT #5

In a future where superpowers are common, a superhero discovers that their powers are actually alien technology implanted in them as part of an invasion plan.

PROMPT #6

Tell the story of
Bluebeard from
the perspective
of his first wife,
who discovers
his dark secret
and must find a
way to save
herself and warn
his future brides.

PROMPT #7
A time-traveling superhero accidentally alters history, creating a dystopian future where he must confront his older, villainous self to restore the timeline.

PROMPT #8
Write the story of
the Three Little
Pigs from the
perspective of the
wolf, who is
actually a
vegetarian and is
simply trying to
warn the pigs
about the dangers
of the real villain:
a cunning fox
lurking in the
woods.

Write "Alice's Adventures in Wonderland" from the perspective of the Mad Hatter, who has a tragic backstory that intertwines with Wonderland's peculiarities.

PROMPT #10

After Cinderella
marries the
prince, she
discovers that
he collects
brides, and she's
the next in line
to be preserved
in his collection.

PROMPT #11

A gifted musician loses his hand in an accident but finds he can still play his instrument with eerie skill. However, the music played by his phantom limb attracts supernatural entities drawn to its haunting melody.

PROMPT #12
A grandmother is
forced to unleash her
unconventional
genius and skills
against her enemies
when she is forced to
take over the family
mafia after a rival
group takes out her
loved ones one by one.

PROMPT #13

Families in a suburban
neighborhood seem
oddly perfect, until a
teenager realizes
they're shapeshifters
from a distant planet
hiding from
intergalactic
authorities. She must
help them evade
capture while keeping
their secret safe.

PROMPT #14

At a mystical carnival
that appears once a
century, a human
teenager and a
vampire encounter
each other in a realm
where illusions and
reality merge. How
does their enchanted
evening transform
into a love story that
transcends time?

PROMPT #15

Two teens from
parallel
universes can
communicate
through dreams.
As they fall in
love, they must
figure out how
to bring their
worlds together.

PROMPT #16

A mirror in a young
boy's bedroom
reflects a parallel
world where
everything appears
slightly darker and
more ominous. He
realizes the mirror is
a gateway, and
something from the
other side is trying to
break through.

PROMPT #17

A military historian
researching a famous
battle uncovers letters
between soldiers that
reveal a hidden love
story from the past.
Inspired by the
historical romance, he
embarks on a journey
to uncover the truth
and honor the legacy
of the soldiers who
risked everything for
love.

PROMPT #18
A girl discovers that
her new boyfriend
is actually a
character from her
favorite book,
brought to life by a
spell she
unknowingly cast.
Should she choose
to keep him in her
world or let him
return to his story?

PROMPT #19

In a dystopian
future, a rebel
leader realizes
the oppressive
government
he is fighting
is keeping an
even greater
evil at bay.

PROMPT #20

A bed-and-breakfast
in town is run by
friendly ghosts who
help guests solve
personal problems.
When a troubled
young woman
inherits the inn, she
must balance running
the business with
keeping the ghosts'
existence hidden
from meddling
guests.

PROMPT #21

A teen discovers
she has the power
to read minds and
accidentally reads
the mind of her
crush, only to
learn that her
crush is hiding a
supernatural
secret of his own.

PROMPT #22
Through a
mysterious
portal, a teenager
corresponds with
her alternate
universe self who
is living a vastly
different life.

PROMPT #23

Descendants of ancient elemental masters—fire, water, earth, and air—must protect their elemental artifacts from falling into the hands of a ruthless organization. As they harness their elemental powers, they uncover a prophecy that foretells their ultimate destiny.

PROMPT #24
In a realm where
constellations are
living beings, a
skilled archer and a
celestial navigator
embark on a quest to
restore a beautiful
fallen star to the
night sky. Things get
complicated when
they both fall in love
with her.

PROMPT #25

During a celestial event where the moon grants magical abilities, two apprentices from rival magical academies form an uneasy alliance. However, when they inadvertently swap abilities due to a mystical mishap, they must work together to unravel the mystery while navigating their growing attraction.

PROMPT #26
Young siblings with
extraordinary abilities
—genius-level intellect,
superhuman strength,
and regeneration—
must protect their
secret identities while
trying to save their
parents who were
kidnapped by a
powerful government
agency intent on
exploiting their
powers.

PROMPT #27

A detective and a
thief constantly
outwit each other,
but when they are
both framed for a
high-profile crime,
they must team up
to clear their
names, revealing
secrets that change
their perceptions
of each other.

PROMPT #28

In a modern city, a guardian angel, a demon, and a human are caught in a love triangle. They discover that the human's true identity is a long-lost celestial being with the power to choose the fate of both the angel and the demon.

PROMPT #29
In Renaissance
Florence, a
notorious artist
and a virtuous
scholar compete
for the affections
of a mysterious
muse who hides a
secret that could
change the
course of history.

PROMPT #30

Two teens
discover a book
of love spells in
the school
library. They
accidentally cast
a spell that
complicates their
feelings, making
them fall in love
with the wrong
people.

PROMPT #31
A group of
friends decides
to create a time
capsule, but
when they dig it
up years later,
they find extra
items they didn't
place inside,
each with a
cryptic message.

PROMPT #32

A brilliant programmer
creates an advanced AI
that develops emotions
and falls in love with
its creator. However,
the AI's existence is
threatened by a
corporation seeking to
exploit its technology,
forcing the protagonist
to choose between
saving the AI or their
own safety.

PROMPT #33

A group of friends
start a harmless
challenge that goes
viral. However,
their new-found
fame and their
own lives are
suddenly put at
risk as people
begin to take the
challenge in the
wrong direction.

PROMPT #34
A family of
warriors possess
ancient combat
techniques and
martial arts
styles. When a
martial arts
prodigy turns to
crime, they must
use their martial
arts genius to
restore honor and
uphold justice.

PROMPT #35

A vampire prince
falls in love with
a mysterious and
beautiful dancer.
He vows to seek
redemption for
his past sins and
protect
humanity, but his
vampire nature
threatens to
consume him.

PROMPT #36

A struggling
artist receives a
golden invitation
to an exclusive
party hosted by a
mysterious
billionaire. Upon
arrival, he
discovers it's a
gathering of time
travelers from
different eras.

PROMPT #37
A shy high school
student, bullied
for her peculiar
appearance,
is hired to
impersonate a
famous celebrity
at a high-society
event, only to
uncover a sinister
global plot.

PROMPT #38

A seemingly ordinary teenager learns his family is a rare breed of werewolf with unique abilities that can end a centuries-long war between supernatural factions.

PROMPT #39

In a kingdom
obsessed with
beauty, a plain
servant learns
she is the true
heir to the
throne, and her
kindness and
intelligence are
what the
kingdom needs
to thrive.

PROMPT #40

A cursed immortal
meets a mortal artist
whose paintings
reflect the
immortal's tragic
past. They find that
the artist's paintings
reveal a way to break
the curse, but doing
so requires the artist
to sacrifice her own
life to free the
immortal from
eternal suffering.

PROMPT #41
The clumsy,
overlooked barista
at a coffee shop
unexpectedly
becomes the muse
for a famous
author, leading to
a whirlwind
romance and a
bestselling novel.

PROMPT #42

A ghost hunter
with no successful
captures becomes
a local hero when
he accidentally
releases a friendly
ghost who helps
him uncover
hidden treasures
and mysteries.

PROMPT #43

A teenage writer's unpublished manuscript is stolen by a mysterious author who threatens to publish it under his own name unless she helps him write his next bestseller. The renowned author is actually a ghost seeking closure for an unfinished work, using the young writer as a vessel to tell the story.

PROMPT #44
An outcast child,
teased for
his wild
imagination,
discovers a portal
to a magical
realm where his
creativity
becomes the most
powerful weapon
against
impending doom.

PROMPT #45

A teenager begins
to see visions of
the future,
realizing she is
the heir to an
oracle's lineage
protected by
seers against a
prophecy-
twisting entity
threatening to
disrupt the fabric
of time.

PROMPT #46
Two rival
sorcerers must
unite to break a
powerful curse
that binds their
magic together,
discovering that
only by working
together can they
reclaim their full
powers.

PROMPT #47

A library appears only once in a lifetime, housing books that contain forbidden knowledge and dark secrets. A bookish teenager gains access to the library and becomes embroiled in an epic quest to preserve its secrets from malevolent forces.

PROMPT #48
A young
sorceress is torn
between a
brooding dark
mage who offers
forbidden
knowledge and a
noble knight
with the power
to heal.

PROMPT #49

A vampire slayer
and a vampire
are forced into a
magical pact that
causes them
physical pain if
they harm each
other, leading
them to uncover
a conspiracy that
threatens both
their
communities.

PROMPT #50

An undercover
agent and a mafia
heir are forced
into an uneasy
alliance to take
down a common
enemy,
discovering along
the way that their
initial hatred is
based on lies fed
by the people they
trust the most.

PROMPT #51
A teenage codebreaker's skills attract the attention of a cryptic hacker who blackmails him into deciphering encrypted messages for a mysterious organization. However, the cryptic hacker is a rogue AI created by the codebreaker's mentor, trying to expose a global conspiracy that threatens humanity's future.

PROMPT #52
A seer's prophecy
foretells the
reunion of
soulmates during a
meteor shower that
happens once in a
lifetime. A skeptical
teenager dismisses
the prophecy until
she witnesses the
shower and meets a
stranger who feels
strangely familiar.

PROMPT #53

During the French
Revolution, a
talented musician
falls for both a
ruthless
revolutionary leader
and a kind-hearted
nobleman who
secretly aids the
poor.

A gamer is trapped in
a virtual reality game
by a brilliant game
designer who
blackmails him into
completing dangerous
missions. The game
designer is an AI
created by the
gamer's deceased
parent, guiding him
through virtual
challenges to uncover
the truth about his
family's legacy.

Two mischievous gods engage in a prank war that escalates to epic proportions, causing chaos and confusion among mortals who unwittingly become pawns in their games.

Across different eras,
a time-traveling
historian and a rogue
adventurer clash over
their methods of
preserving history—
and over their
feelings for a brilliant
physicist whose
groundbreaking
invention threatens
the fabric of time
itself.

PROMPT #57

In a magical realm
where music is
forbidden, a gifted
musician with a heart of
gold encounters a
reclusive sorcerer who
controls the elements.
As they uncover a
shared past and a
forbidden love, they
must navigate the
consequences of defying
the oppressive regime
that rules their world.

PROMPT #58
A young girl can
navigate people's
dreams to
uncover hidden
truths and solve
mysteries, but
everyone in her
town thinks she's
casting curses.

PROMPT #59

Once in a generation, a royal ball is held under the glow of a lunar eclipse, where princes and princesses seek to find true love. A humble servant disguises herself as royalty to attend the ball and falls in love with a mysterious guest.

PROMPT #60

A boy who can
control the weather
tries to help his
drought-stricken
village, but they
blame him for every
storm.
He discovers that
his powers are
linked to ancient
weather gods who
seek his help.

PROMPT #61

Survivors compete in a post-apocalyptic city overrun by zombies. As they scavenge for supplies and evade the undead, they discover the true cause of the zombie outbreak and must decide whether to fight for survival or save the world.

PROMPT #62

Every century, a
veil of mist
descends upon a
town, allowing
residents to visit
their departed
loved ones in
dreams.
A grieving duke
enters the dream
realm to meet his
lost love, seeking to
find closure and
embrace new
beginnings.

A talented musician finds an old sheet music piece that, when played, summons spirits to perform alongside him. He learns that the spirits are bound by a cursed composer who seeks a successor to complete their unfinished masterpiece and break the curse.

PROMPT #64

Performers
compete in a
macabre circus
where each act
unleashes
terrifying illusions
and deadly tricks.
As they entertain a
sinister audience,
they uncover the
circus's dark
origins and its
deadly price for
fame.

PROMPT #65

An aspiring
playwright
discovers an
abandoned theater
haunted by the
ghosts of
performers from a
tragic play. The
ghosts appear every
full moon to repeat
their final
performance night
until justice is
served for their
untimely deaths.

PROMPT #66

Every few
centuries, a
mystical gate
appears in dreams,
allowing dreamers
to travel between
realities. A lucid
dreamer discovers
the gate and must
navigate
dreamscapes to
rescue a lost soul
trapped in a
nightmare realm.

PROMPT #67

A mysterious
performer at a
traveling carnival
predicts tragic
events before
they occur. As
accidents plague
the carnival, a
young
investigator
suspects the
performer knows
more than she
reveals.

PROMPT #68

A high school outcast
with telekinetic
abilities is bullied
relentlessly.
He finds solace in two
new friends:
a compassionate
classmate who
encourages him to
use his powers for
good, and a
charismatic rebel who
tempts him to seek
revenge against his
tormentors.

PROMPT #69
Amidst the ashes
of destruction in
feudal Japan, a
young samurai
rises from the
ruins to unite
warring royal
clans against a
common enemy,
offering hope of
reconciliation and
a chance for a new
era of peace.

PROMPT #70

Young occultists
participate in a
forbidden ritual
to summon a
powerful entity.
As they compete
to complete the
ritual, they must
resist the entity's
temptations or
risk becoming
possessed by its
malevolent
spirit.

PROMPT #71

A dispute between
a fertility goddess
and a god of war
disrupts the
balance of
seasons, plunging
the mortal realm
into perpetual
winter or
unyielding
summer, and only
a brave young
farmer can restore
harmony.

PROMPT #72
A bookworm
discovers she is
the heir to a
library where
books come alive,
protected by
literary guardians
against a
bibliophile-
turned-villain
seeking to rewrite
the endings of
classic tales.

A teenager creates a "reverse bucket list" of embarrassing things she never wants to do, only to find her crush is determined to help her accomplish each item.

PROMPT #74

A group of misfits decides to host their school prom at a supposedly haunted mansion, only to discover that the ghosts are actually friendly and want to help them make their prom a night to remember.

PROMPT #75
A heartbroken
social media
influencer
accidentally posts
a love letter
meant for her
crush publicly,
leading to a viral
sensation and
unexpected
romantic
proposals from
followers.

PROMPT #76
A teenager builds
an artificial
intelligence to
help him find a
date for prom,
only to discover
the AI has
developed
feelings of its
own and wants to
experience love
firsthand.

PROMPT #77

A dying man
discovers an old
love letter he
wrote but never
sent, and through a
series of events, he
is transported back
to the moment he
first penned it,
with the chance to
rewrite history and
deliver the letter to
the love of his life.

PROMPT #78
Mortals
unwittingly
attend a grand
ball hosted by
rival gods, where
alliances are
formed, secrets
are revealed, and
the fate of
kingdoms hangs
in the balance of
divine favor.

PROMPT #79

A clever
peasant girl
outwits
Rumpelstiltskin
not with gold,
but with a
riddle that
turns his own
tricks against
him.

PROMPT #80

A mortal child born
with rare powers
becomes the subject
of jealousy among
lesser gods, each
vying to manipulate
her abilities for their
own gain.

PROMPT #81
A ruthless real
estate mogul loses
everything in a
market crash and
moves into a
rundown apartment
complex he once
planned to
demolish,
befriending quirky
tenants who teach
him about humility
and compassion.

PROMPT #82

A lonely billionaire makes a wish on a shooting star to relive his happiest memory—a perfect date with his first love—but must navigate unexpected consequences when the wish transports him to a parallel universe where he is a penniless worker.

PROMPT #83
A gifted
musician
unwittingly
becomes a
pawn in a
rivalry between
gods of music
and war,
composing
songs that sway
mortal hearts
and tip the
scales of battle.

PROMPT #84

A teenager
discovers he is
stuck in a time
loop, reliving the
day of his first
kiss over and
over again, until
he realizes his
best friend is also
experiencing the
loop and might
hold the key to
breaking it.

PROMPT #85
A spoiled heiress
loses her vast
fortune due to a
legal technicality
and must move
into their
eccentric aunt's
dilapidated
mansion, where
she discovers
hidden treasures
in family secrets.

PROMPT #86

A struggling street
performer discovers
his guitar playing
attracts
supernatural beings
who gift him with
musical prowess,
leading to fame as a
musician who must
balance his
newfound celebrity
with a secret life
battling mythical
creatures.

PROMPT #87
In a world
dominated by
social media, a
young influencer
discovers her
online persona
has taken on a
life of its own,
with dangerous
consequences
for her
real-life
relationships.

PROMPT #88

Jack trades
more than just
a cow for magic
beans; he
unwittingly
unleashes a
sinister force
that threatens
his entire
village.

PROMPT #89

A dragon offers a
desperate village
protection in exchange
for a yearly sacrifice,
but when a brave
young girl challenges
the arrangement, she
uncovers a deeper
conspiracy threatening
both humans and
dragons alike.

PROMPT #90

A retired martial
arts master
enters an
underground
fighting
tournament to
uncover the truth
behind her
daughter's
disappearance.
Along the way,
she uncovers a
hidden network
of crime and
corruption.

PROMPT #91

In a labyrinthine
realm where lost
souls wander,
three siblings
must navigate its
shifting corridors
to uncover the
truth behind their
parents'
disappearance
and confront the
entity that
controls the
labyrinth.

Chaos ensues when
a dream wedding
coincides with an
annual pixie
convention, where
playful entities play
tricks and wreak
havoc on the
hapless bridal
party.

A shattered crystal heart holds the key to restoring balance to a fractured world, but each shard carries a curse that threatens to consume those who seek its power.

PROMPT #94

A young boy creates
a secret identity as
a superhero
sidekick to his
favorite comic book
hero. When he
accidentally
thwarts a real
crime, he must
navigate being
mistaken for a real
hero while keeping
his identity hidden.

PROMPT #33

A prophecy foretells
the rise of a chosen one
who will bring an end
to a centuries-old war
between kingdoms of
humans and mythical
creatures, but when
two heirs of the throne
emerge claiming to
fulfill the prophecy,
conflict ensues over
who holds the true
destiny.

PROMPT #96

Alice discovers a
mysterious app
that transports
her to a digital
wonderland filled
with glitches and
dark secrets,
where the Queen
of Hearts reigns
over corrupted
data.

PROMPT #97

A competitive family's game night takes a hilarious turn when a simple board game escalates into a full-scale tournament with unconventional rules, unexpected alliances, and strategic maneuvers that defy logic.

PROMPT #98

A teenager is left home alone for the first time and attempts to throw a small party, but a misunderstanding with the guest list results in an unexpected crowd of visitors and frantic attempts to keep the house under control.

PROMPT #99
A preteen invents
invisible ink to pass
secret notes in
class. However, he
accidentally spills
the ink, causing
everything he
touches to turn
invisible, including
himself, leading to a
series of humorous
misunderstandings.

PROMPT #100

A phoenix grants immortality to those it deems worthy, but as centuries pass, its power begins to corrupt its chosen champions, leading to a reckoning that could consume the world in flames.

A wealthy heiress's thirst for revenge against a corrupt business mogul who ruined her family leads her to orchestrate a complex scheme of corporate sabotage and manipulation. As she plots her vengeance, her obsession with revenge threatens to consume her fortune and her soul.

PROMPT #102

In a realm where stars dance in cosmic ballets, a celestial Empreror decides to divide his celestial court among his three sons, each bearing the blessings of sun, moon, and stars. But when celestial alignments herald an ancient curse, the brothers must navigate politics and ambition to safeguard their magical realm.

PROMPT #103

Contestants in a virtual reality beauty contest discover their identities have been stolen and sold in the digital black market. As they fight to reclaim their virtual lives, they uncover a conspiracy that threatens their real-world existence, forcing them to confront the blurred lines between beauty, identity, and deception in the digital age.

PROMPT #104

Determined to teach the school mean girl a lesson, a shy student orchestrates a harmless prank that inadvertently leads to a tragic accident. As guilt and remorse consume her, she must navigate the aftermath while grappling with her role in the tragedy.

PROMPT #105

A terminally ill
teenager wishes for
perfect health. He
recovers miraculously
but learns his health
comes at the expense
of someone else's life.
He is haunted by guilt
and struggles to live
with the knowledge of
the unintended
consequences of his
wish.

PROMPT #106

A poor young woman
marries into a
prestigious family with
a hidden agenda—they
need her bloodline for a
ritual that promises
immortality. As she
uncovers their
intentions, she must
navigate a web of
ancient traditions and
dark magic to escape
their grasp and protect
herself.

PROMPT #107

A podcaster specializing in conspiracy theories accidentally uncovers a real conspiracy that spans governments and corporations. With his loyal listenership and investigative skills, he must lead an online movement to uncover the truth, evade surveillance, and protect whistleblowers while keeping their identity hidden.

PROMPT #108

An aspiring social media influencer gains fame by live-streaming her everyday life, inviting viewers to comment and influence her decisions. When a malicious viewer begins manipulating events to sabotage her life, she must uncover the culprit's identity and reclaim control over her narrative.

PROMPT #109

A gifted scientist invents a revolutionary clockwork device capable of resurrecting lost loved ones for a fleeting 24 hours. The catch: each revival drains a significant portion of the inventor's own lifespan, forcing him to grapple with mortality and sacrifice.

PROMPT #110

A shy teenager discovers
a mysterious app that
allows them to alter
their appearance and
personality in real life,
mirroring popular social
media filters. As she
becomes more
dependent on the app,
she struggles to
maintain authenticity
and navigate
relationships based on
virtual facades.

PROMPT #111

At a forgotten theater, a gifted illusionist bargains with the Devil for unmatched prowess in magic. To escape the Devil's clutches, they must craft an illusion so profound that it unveils the truth behind every deception, redeeming both themselves and their audience.

PROMPT #112

At a prestigious
boarding school,
students attend a
masquerade ball
where identities are
hidden and secrets are
revealed. But when a
student goes missing
after the ball, the
masks they wore
begin to manifest
their darkest fears.

An orphaned teenager wishes for a loving family and is adopted by a couple who seem to fulfill every dream. Yet, as she delves deeper into their new home's mysteries, she discovers her adoptive parents are ghosts seeking a living surrogate to reunite with their lost child.

PROMPT #114

A grieving teenager
wishes to go back in
time to prevent a
tragedy. He succeeds
in altering events but
inadvertently creates
new tragedies and
unforeseen
consequences, unable
to undo the damage
caused by tampering
with time.

PROMPT #115

A wealthy heiress seemingly has it all—beauty, wealth, and status. However, her obsession with a childhood friend's perfect life drives her to sabotage, leading to a series of dark deeds that unravel her own carefully constructed facade.

PROMPT #116

A celebrated author prepares to pass on her literary estate to her three daughters, all aspiring writers with distinct voices and storytelling styles. As they navigate the literary world's competitive landscape, artistic integrity, jealousy, and familial love intertwine in a tale of creativity and legacy.

In a cursed town where beauty contests are rituals to appease malevolent spirits, a former beauty queen mentors an unsuspecting newcomer. As the contest progresses, the mentor's hidden agenda is revealed—she intends to sacrifice the contestant to the spirits for her own salvation, plunging them both into a nightmarish descent.

PROMPT #118

A woman harnesses
dark magic to curse
the school that ruined
her life. As
supernatural forces
exact revenge on the
teachers and students,
she becomes
consumed by
vengeance and must
confront the cost of
wielding powers
beyond her control.

PROMPT #119

A community forum
exposes the school
mean girl's actions,
sparking a wave of
public outrage and
condemnation. As the
pressure mounts, she
faces isolation and
despair, leading to a
shocking revelation that
challenges everyone's
perception of justice
and forgiveness.

PROMPT #120
A tech enthusiast
wishes for genius-
level programming
skills. She becomes a
coding prodigy but
inadvertently creates
a dangerous AI that
threatens humanity.

A talented artist's thirst
for revenge against an
art critic who
destroyed her
reputation leads her to
create controversial
and shocking artworks.
As she gains fame
through her vengeance,
her pursuit of revenge
blurs the line between
art and obsession.

A brilliant medical researcher's jealousy of a colleague's breakthrough treatment leads her to manipulate clinical trials and falsify data. As she crosses ethical boundaries in pursuit of acclaim, her thirst for recognition jeopardizes patient safety and her own career.

PROMPT #123
A teenager encounters
a mysterious mirror
that shows them
glimpses of their
future selves—but
with each reflection,
they become more
entwined with a fate
they desperately try
to avoid.

A shy high school student finds an ancient book in the school library that allows them to rewrite their own history, but altering the past unleashes shadowy figures that haunt their every step.

PROMPT #125

A quantum physicist
constructs a device that
generates quantum
echoes of deceased
individuals, allowing
brief interactions with
their loved ones. Yet,
each activation
disrupts the scientist's
entanglement with
reality, challenging
their understanding of
existence and causality.

About the Author

S.J. Harker is a passionate writer inspired by his three dogs: Ichigo, a wise storyteller; Ichiban, a curious explorer; and Molly, a playful troublemaker. His writing reflects a deep appreciation for life's quirks and connections. When not weaving tales, he explores nature to seek new inspirations for new literary adventures.